How to Wire Electrical Outlets, Switches, and Lights

TEXT BY DEANNE RAFFEL

A WALL
Published by Simon & Schuster
New York

Published by WALLABY BOOKS
A Simon & Schuster Division of
GULF & WESTERN CORPORATION
Simon & Schuster Building
1230 Avenue of the Americas
New York, New York 10020

WALLABY and colophon are trademarks
of Simon & Schuster

First Wallaby Books Printing May, 1981

10   9   8   7   6   5   4   3   2   1

Manufactured in the United States of America

Library of Congress Catalogue Card Number: 80-26658

ISBN: 0-671- 42309-6

The advice in this book is based on careful research
and analysis. Due care should be taken in any repair
or maintenance program. The author and publisher
cannot take any responsibility for damage or injuries
caused by repairs or maintenance performed by
the reader.

Production: Jeffrey Weiss Group, Inc./Color Book Design, Inc.
Series Editor: Edward P. Stevenson
Design: Deborah Bracken, Design Director
Design Consultant: Robert Luzzi
Managing Editor: Barbara Frontera
Copy Chief: Donna Florence
Illustrated by: Ray Skibinski
Special Thanks to Jack Artenstein, Eugene Brissie, Jenny Doctorow and
Channa Taub

Table of Contents

Introduction

There is nothing more frustrating than having a breakdown in some part of the electrical system in your home—whether it be a lamp, an extension cord, or a switch. Calling in an electrician usually is an expensive and time-consuming affair. But many electrical repairs don't require the services of an electrician—all they need is someone who has a basic knowledge of how electrical components function.

So why not be the trouble-shooter in your house? Find the problem and rectify it! You need not be particularly "handy." On the following pages are very elementary repairs that *you* can do. Your electrical system is described and illustrated, the necessary tools and materials are shown, step-by-step instructions are supplied. Read the copy thoroughly, study the diagrams dealing with your problems carefully, obtain the required tools and materials, and go to work. Just remember to follow ALL directions in sequence.

Your first attempts will probably take time and this is good and proper. Caution is a wise watchword when you are trying to do something new. If you rush, you may well become frustrated and "mess up." But once you have successfully completed your first project, you will become more confident and go on to try others. The satisfaction of becoming the "fix-it" person in your house cannot be described in words, and achieving independence from the waiting—and paying—game of having to depend on service people for minor repairs is really a major accomplishment.

Electricity in the Home

E lectricity plays such a large role in our everyday life that without it we would be both literally and figuratively in the dark. We must treat it with respect; it has the potential to do harm as well as good if it is not handled carefully and responsibly.

Electricity is all around us, though it has no color, size, weight or smell. Occasionally, we see it as lightning or feel it as static when we remove clothes from the dryer. But what, exactly, is it?

Defining Electricity

To define **electric current**—the kind of electricity we *use*—on an elementary level, it is the flow of tiny subatomic particles called *electrons* along a *conductor*. Your electrical system is in many respects like your water supply system; turn on a tap, or switch, and out it runs. Just as current in a river is the flow of water within the banks of the river, current in electricity is the flow of electrons along a conductor.

Electricity is produced commercially in a power plant or generating station from some other form of energy—fossil, mechanical (hydroelectric), or nuclear. From the generating station it travels over a network of wires that distribute it to various communities. From a transformer located near your house, the current is delivered through overhead or underground wires into your building, through an electric meter and then to your home's electrical center, the service panel or box. From the service panel, the electricity travels to the fixtures and outlets of your home by means of a series of *branch circuits*.

A **conductor** is *any* material through which electricity *will travel*. Many materials are conductors of electricity: various metals, tap water—even people, unfortunately (more on that later). The term is usually *used* to mean "good" or efficient conductor. The conductors most in use in the electrical industry are copper and aluminium *wires*. Some materials are very poor conductors; they are called **insulators**. Rubber, plastic and asbestos are all very good insulators and are used to sheath electrical wires and prevent the current from escaping from its intended conductor to an unintended one, such as yourself.

Measuring Electricity

The following terms are the names of units of measurement for electrical current.

• **Voltage** (the units are called **volts**) is the force or *pressure* that gets the electrons moving to create the current. Think of it in the same terms as water entering your house under a given measurable pressure.

• **Amperage** (the units are called **amps** or **amperes**) is the measure of the *amount of cur-*

rent being used—actually the number of electrons that pass a given point per second. Equate amps with gallons of water per minute. Many electrical components are "rated" in amps; the rating identifies the largest amount of current they can *safely* carry.

• **Wattage** (the units are called **watts**) is the measure of the *amount of power* being used. It is a product of voltage multiplied by amperage. Light bulbs and most other electrical appliances are labeled with the number of watts of power they consume.

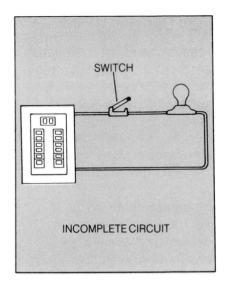

INCOMPLETE CIRCUIT

Circuits

Electrical current flows in a circle. For current to flow, there must be a continuous connection from the power source to the "load" or device being powered, and back to the source. Any interruption in this "circuit," and electricity stops flowing.

The circuit is usually a system of conductors (wires), insulated from the surrounding environment, leading from the source (the generating station) to the appliance and back to the source. One or two more switches are usually incorporated into the circuit along the way so that it

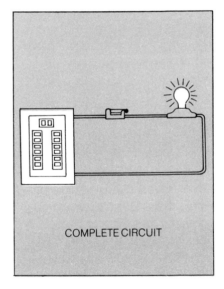

COMPLETE CIRCUIT

can be opened (turned off) or closed (turned on) at will. The current stays within the insulated wires and everything remains safe.

Short Circuits

In cases where current *escapes* from the system of conductors in which it is supposed to run, for example, because of frayed, broken or inappropriately exposed wires, danger arises. When electricity travels through an unintentional path—when it escapes from the intended path— a **short circuit** has occurred. Short circuits can cause sparks to fly, and if *you* should inadvertently become part of the short circuit, you will

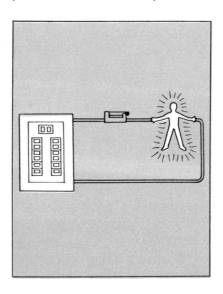

experience electric shock. Most of the safety rules in this book are designed to keep you from *ever* becoming part of an electric circuit.

Service, New and Old

A modern residential electrical service provides a three-wire system capable of supplying electric current at either 120 or 240 volts. Two of the three wires are "hot" supply wires, each carrying current at 120 volts. The third wire is the "neutral" wire which completes the circuit back to the source.

Many major electrical appliances, such as cooking ranges and clothes dryers, run much more efficiently at higher voltages, hence the necessity of 240-volt household wiring capacity. We will not be concerned with 240-volt situations in this book, but that is no reason not to understand them. A 240-volt device has a three-pronged plug. Each of the two main prongs engages a connection with one of the two 120-volt lines. The third prong makes the connection with the neutral. (An old-fashioned two-wire system that supplies current at 120 volts through one "hot" wire and one neutral wire can be updated by the utility company's bringing in an additional 120-volt "hot" wire.

The Service Panel

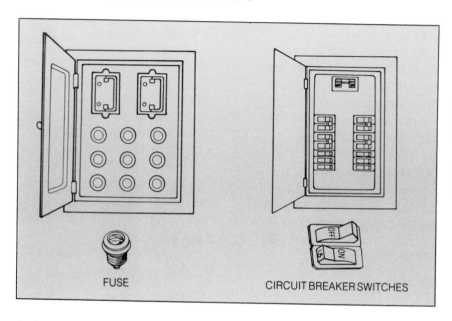

FUSE   CIRCUIT BREAKER SWITCHES

At the service panel, the current is distributed to the various "house circuits" or "branch circuits." Each of these circuits is equipped with either a **circuit breaker**, or a **fuse**, depending on the system's age. (They serve exactly the same function, the only practical difference is that fuses can only be used once and must be thrown away when they blow.) Each fuse or circuit breaker is rated to carry a certain load of current, indicated in the number of amps printed on the top of the fuse or on the breaker switch. If the total current (number of amperes) drawn by the electrical equipment (lights, tools, appliances, etc.) operating on the circuit exceeds the rating of that particular fuse or breaker, the fuse will "blow" or the breaker will "trip," *shutting off the circuit*. This is a protective action that prevents circuit wiring from overheating. (If a wire is not capable of carrying the load imposed on it, it will overheat and can cause the insulation to deteriorate or actually burn. Serious fires can result.)

When a breaker trips or a fuse blows, **find out why** before you reset or replace it. The two most likely causes are (1) a short circuit resulting from a deteriorated lamp cord or other exposed wire and (2) simply overloading the circuit by operating too many devices on it at one time. (Heating appliances such as irons and portable heaters are the biggest power gobblers and often the culprits in overload situations.) Locate the short circuit and unplug the lamp or appliance in question, or turn off some of the "loads" on the circuit before you reset the breaker or replace the fuse.

If you *cannot* identify the problem and/or if the circuit goes out repeatedly, CALL AN ELECTRICIAN.

To reset a circuit breaker, simply flip the switch back to ON. (On some breakers, you must first push the switch further in the OFF direction, then flip it ON.)

To replace a fuse, simply unscrew it from its socket and replace it with a new one *of the same amperage rating*.

Turning Off The Power

Besides acting as safety devices, the fuses or circuit breakers in your service panel are the switches that you will use to turn off the current on a house circuit

breaker whenever you do *any work* that involves exposing or touching the circuit wiring. Turning off the power at the panel box is called "killing the circuit" in the trade.

In addition to the breakers or fuses for the branch circuits, each service panel has a switch or some means of turning off all current to the entire house. This main shut-off will be in the form

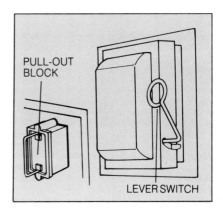

PULL-OUT BLOCK

LEVER SWITCH

of a main breaker switch in modern boxes. In older fuse-type services, there may be either a lever switch that turns the power off when it is moved so as to disengage the "knife" from the contacts or a "pull-out block" that contains cartridge fuses. None of the projects in this book will require you to shut off the house power altogether, but in certain kinds of emergencies it may be required.

Be Safe, Not Sorry

There are several types of safety controls imposed on electrical equipment and installations by governmental and other authorities.

The major control is the National Electrical Code (NEC), sponsored by the National Fire Protection Association. It has laid down standards for electrical safety by establishing a set of rules (the Code) that controls the mechanics of installations. (The 1981 Code covers 681 pages.) The NEC is reviewed and updated every three years.

Local codes are also established to supplement or in certain instances to refute the NEC. To go even further, most municipalities require a permit for any significant wiring installation. The work is almost always to be performed by a licensed electrician. (An electrician must take and pass a difficult test based on the NEC and local codes before being issued a license by a municipality.) Electrical inspectors then check the work for which a permit was given to be sure that it was performed according to the NEC and local code.

Testing

All material used in electrical installations must be "approved by" a nationally recognized testing laboratory such as Underwriters Laboratories, Inc. (This particular testing laboratory is the one that we are most familiar with.) A "UL Listed" item has been tested and approved for use *under certain conditions* which include *correct installation* according to the Code.

Grounding

The earlier statement that an electrical circuit *must* run from the power source to the load or fixture and *back to the original source* was a slight oversimplification. The earth or **ground** also has the capacity to serve as the completing link in an electrical circuit. In other words, if you are connected to a "hot" conductor *and* also to the ground in some fashion or other the current will flow through you into the ground. This holds true for any conductor.

Therefore, modern electrical codes require that all appliances and every part of your electrical system be "grounded" or connected efficiently to the earth so that, if any current *does* escape due to a short circuit or any other cause, it will have an easy and harmless path to follow, reducing the danger of shock to you.

The initial grounding of your residential electrical system is accomplished when the electrician who installs the service runs a heavy gauge "house ground" wire from your service panel to a

HOUSE GROUND
CONNECTION

"grounding electrode"—either a metal rod driven into the earth or a metal water pipe that is buried in the ground. In turn, there must be a continuous connection from every outlet box in the house to the panel box, and, ultimately, to the house ground.

So, in actuality, in an old-fashioned two-wire system there are actually *three conductors* running throughout the system: one "hot" supply wire connected to the power source, one "neutral" wire leading back to the source, and a continuous conductor — not necessarily a wire, but often made up of the boxes and the metal-sheathed cable that connects them — to the ground. A modern three-wire system actually contains *four conductors*: two hot supply wires, one neutral wire and a continuous ground. In up-to-date installations the measures taken to insure proper grounding of all the elements of electrical systems have become more stringent and more elaborate than they were in the past.

Color-Coding

One of the ways that the National Electrical Code helps to insure the safety of those who work with electricity is that it requires manufacturers to color-code the conductors in the various kinds of electrical cables they make.

• In a two-wire, metal-sheathed cable, the "hot" wire is always black, the neutral wire always white.

• In a so-called two-wire plastic-sheathed cable there are actually three wires: a black hot wire, a white neutral wire and a bare copper ground wire.

• In a three-wire metal-sheathed cable, there are two hot wires — one black, one red — and a white neutral wire.

• In a so-called three-wire plastic-sheathed cable there are four conductors: a black and a red hot wire, a white neutral wire and a bare copper ground wire.

It is now required by the code that all receptacles be grounded specifically and directly to the boxes in which they are housed *by means of a separate wire*. This (and any other grounding wire) is always coded green.

Safety Tips

Since electricity has the power to harm as well as help, your main concern when working with it should be SAFETY FIRST. **Never take any risks** when attempting electrical work. If you are not absolutely sure of what you are doing, don't try it. AL-WAYS shut off the power to any electrical device you are going to work on. If it is a lamp or appliance, UNPLUG it. If it is a switch, receptacle or fixture, KILL THE CIRCUIT. As long as you are absolutely sure the power is off, you can proceed. These rules are so important that they are restated below, along with a number of others.

1. Never work on any electrical device unless the power is SHUT OFF. Always double check by *testing* to be sure that the power is indeed off.

2. Always UNPLUG a lamp or other appliance before working on it.

3. Never use an appliance or tool that has a cracked or frayed cord. If the conductors are exposed, you may receive a shock.

4. Always REPLACE a cracked or frayed lamp cord or extension cord.

5. Never pull on the cord when unplugging an appliance from a receptacle; that puts unnecessary mechanical stress on the connection. Grasp the PLUG and pull it out.

6. Never touch an electrical fixture or device with WET hands or wet clothing. Moisture improves the conductivity of many materials, including yourself, and increases the danger of shock.

7. Never use an electric tool outdoors when the earth is wet. Again, MOISTURE increases conductivity and increases danger of shock.

8. If your service panel is in a damp location, stand on a board whenever working on it. The board serves as an INSULATOR.

9. Always wear RUBBER-SOLED shoes when using an electric tool outside or when working in the panel box or any electrical box. The rubber soles are effective insulators.

10. Never touch (with your body) a faucet, pipes or any other part of the plumbing system, the gas lines or the heating system when working with electric tools or when doing work on the electrical system. These are all effective GROUNDS, which will make it easier for electric current to flow through your body.

11. Never touch the panel box with both hands at the same time. Never touch the box with one hand and touch an adjacent pipe or wall at the same time. Always keep one hand FREE to avoid grounding yourself.

Tools and Materials

When you're doing any type of repair work around your home, having the proper tools for the job at hand makes all the difference between a pleasant, satisfying experience and exasperating frustration. There are general tools that almost everyone has around and some more specialized ones, designed to do specific tasks. You may have to buy a few specialized tools to do electrical work efficiently. Do not scrimp when it comes to buying tools. Buy what you need, and buy *good* tools. A well-made tool is a pleasure to use and will usually give years of service. "Bargain" tools are in reality no bargain at all. They tend to be junk, made from inferior materials and poorly machined, a real *waste* of money.

Tools

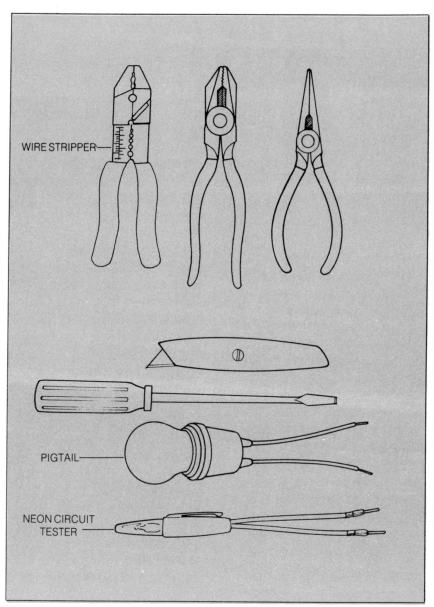

WIRE STRIPPER

PIGTAIL

NEON CIRCUIT TESTER

You will need the following tools to do basic electrical work:

a selection of screwdrivers— at least one large and one small standard-blade driver and one Phillips type

- "lineman's" pliers

- long-nose ("needle-nose") pliers

- wire strippers

- pigtail lampholder and light bulb *or* neon circuit tester

- utility knife

- pocket knife

Screwdrivers should be in good condition. That means the flat-bladed ones should be clean with square, properly ground tips, not chewed up from misuse. Likewise for the Phillips. Screwdrivers are not so expensive that they can't be replaced from time to time.

Two types of **pliers** make it easier for you to do a variety of jobs efficiently. The long-nosed pair is handy for bending wire loops and getting into tight spots. The lineman's pliers are sturdier—good for loosening nuts, cutting wire, etc.

Wire strippers are a type of scissors made for cutting and stripping wire. On some types, the cutting blades adjust by means of a screw setting to accommodate wires of different gauge sizes. Other types have separate cutting notches for the different gauges. Set properly or using the proper notch, the stripper will cut the proper depth through the *insulation* without cutting into the conductor (wire).

A **pigtail lampholder** (with a bulb that you know is functioning) serves as a test lamp to verify the "electrical condition" of devices—that is, whether or not current is flowing to or through them. A **neon-bulb circuit tester** does the same job but is not as easy to see as an incandescent bulb in a pigtail.

A **utility knife** belongs in any toolbox, so if you don't have one already, get one now. You will use it to cut materials such as plastic insulation on electric cable. The blades are easily and inexpensively replaced when they become dull. (Utility knives should be used for cutting only, *never* for prying, as the blades are quite brittle and shear off easily.)

It is a good idea to keep a pocket knife handy too. The blade is both longer and stronger than that of a utility knife.

Materials

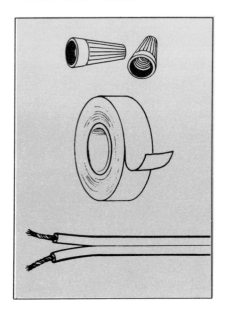

The list of materials that you will use in your basic electrical work is not extensive; it consists of:

- wire nuts
- electrical tape
- lamp cord

Wire nuts, also called **solderless connectors**, take the place of both solder *and* electrical tape in many instances. Their purpose is to connect and secure the ends of wires in a firm mechanical bond. The housing is made of plastic and inside it is a helically wound spring that acts very much like an interior thread. When the wire nut is placed over the ends of the wires to be connected and turned clockwise, the spring tightens its hold on the wires, holding them securely. The beauty of wire nuts is that they act both as connectors and as insulators *and* they are as easy to remove as to install.

A roll of **electrical tape** should always be handy. It is used to cover exposed wires in several kinds of situations such as splicing in which a wire nut cannot be used. The older type known as friction tape is acceptable and has the advantage that it can be torn from the roll. The newer PVC plastic tape is much tougher and must be cut with a knife.

Two-strand **lamp cord** is available, generally, in two colors, white and brown, and several sizes or *gauges*. (Wire gauge numbers are an arbitrary set of numbers applied to wires of different electrical carrying capacities or, ultimately, sizes. Oddly enough, the smaller the gauge number, the larger the wire or conductor.) The most common gauge of lamp cord is #18, but you may also want to purchase the heavier #16 cord, for use in making up extension cords, for example.

Your Electrical System

While we are on the subject of wire and wire gauges, we might just as well take a look at the principal types of cables that make the branch circuits inside the walls of your house. There are three main possibilities:

• Steel armored (metal-sheathed) cable, known in the trade as "BX" cable in which two or more plastic insulated conductors run, along with a thin "bonding wire."

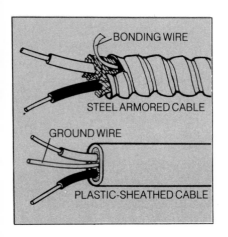

BONDING WIRE

STEEL ARMORED CABLE

GROUND WIRE

PLASTIC-SHEATHED CABLE

• Plastic-sheathed cable, known most commonly in the trade by the name "Romex"—which is a trademark of a par-

ticular manufacturer's version of the product—in which two or more plastic insulated conductors run, along with a bare copper ground wire.

• A "conduit" system, consisting of metal pipes in which run the appropriate number of plastic insulated conductors. In a conduit system, the conduit itself acts as the grounding conductor, as does the metal armor of the BX cable.

The gauges of interior house wires in fairly recent installations will be #14, or, in some cases, the heavier #12. In older installations you may find the thinner #16 gauge wire, often in a deteriorating fabric insulator. If this is the case in your home, it is probably time to be thinking about a major rewiring job (not a do-it-yourself project).

Outlet Boxes

Lurking behind the cover plates of light switches, receptacles and light fixtures are metal boxes that house the devices in question. The metal **outlet box** has been part of residential wiring virtually from the beginning. The box houses and protects its contents and serves as part of

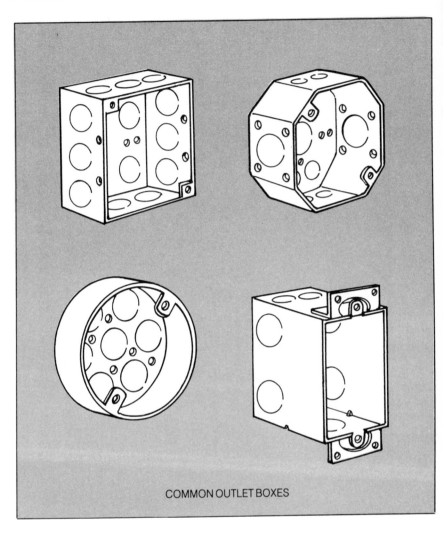

COMMON OUTLET BOXES

the continuous ground conductor (see p. 13). Different box sizes and shapes have been used at different times and for different purposes. Some have built-in clamps for securing the cables that run in and out of them. Some have separate connectors that attach to the box through round "knock-outs," available in various locations around the box. The most common types—the ones you are most likely to encounter in your own electrical work—are pictured here.

Making a Circuit Diagram

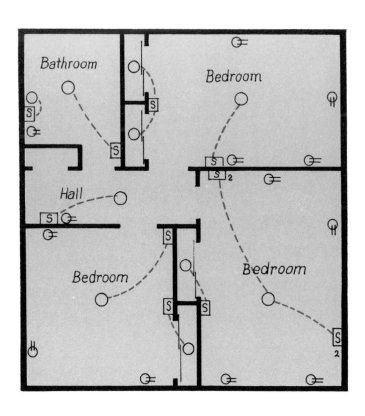

S	SINGLE-POLE SWITCH
₂S	3-WAY SWITCH
⌐	DUPLEX RECEPTACLE
○	LIGHT FIXTURE
- - - -	LIGHT SWITCH CONNECTION

It is important to know which circuit in your panel box controls each particular electrical device or appliance in your house. When you want to do any repair or replacement work, it is clearly more sensible to kill only the circuit that leads to the device in question than to shut off the main switch. You need a **circuit diagram** that will instantly give the information required.

To begin, number each circuit breaker or fuse in the service panel. Then draw the floor plans of your house, including the attic, garage and basement. Use a separate sheet of paper for each floor. Indicate each ceiling and wall fixture, wall switches controlling these lights (shown by a dotted line running from the switches to the fixture), receptacles, and large appliances that are permanent installations.

To find which circuit controls which light, do as follows:

1. Work with a partner. One person will control the circuits at the panel (the controller) while the other person works the switches and lights in a room (the receiver).

2. Work on one room at a time. Turn on all lights, plug a lamp or small appliance that is turned ON (vacuum, radio, clock set on alarm, etc.) into every receptacle.

3. The controller begins by switching OFF and ON power on each individual circuit until the receiver yells "Stop" when a light or other device goes out in the room.

4. The controller informs the receiver of the number of the circuit that is switched OFF. The receiver, in turn, records the appropriate symbol for each device that has been disabled by the dead circuit, in the appropriate location on the floor plan and indicates the circuit number on each. There will be considerable yelling back and forth before all the devices in the house are covered. (A house or dwelling that is properly and adequately wired will not have every device in any one room on a single circuit.)

5. Most receptacles have two outlet plugs. Each should be circuit-tested since they might not be wired on the same line. Also remember to check all wall switches and the single fixture that they control.

6. Protect the diagram sheets in acetate envelopes. Keep them near the service box so they can be called on when needed.

Extension Cords

The familiar household extension cord is one of the simplest electrical devices that we use—a two-wire conductor with a fitting at either end to allow it to be connected to a power source and to an appliance.

Extension cords can be purchased, of course, but there are two reasons that you might want to make your own. First, you can save a bit of money. Second, you can customize them— make them just the right length for the situation at hand and avoid having many feet of unneeded wire cluttering up your rooms. In addition, you can salvage and repair any commercially produced extension that may have been damaged accidently. (An old cord in which the insulation has deteriorated should simply be discarded.)

According to the NEC, a flexible extension should NEVER be snaked through holes in walls, ceilings or floors. Its purpose is only to reach from a receptacle to a lamp or appliance that is too far away for its own cord to reach.

Tools and Materials

- wire cutters

- 18-gauge lamp cord in the color of your choice

- patent, easy-attaching plugs, "male" and "female"

Making and Repairing Two-Wire Cords

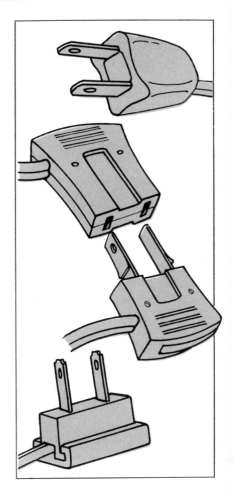

Making a Custom Cord

1. Measure the distance you want your cord to cover. Make sure the cord will be long enough to hang slack. Cut your 18-gauge lamp cord to the length you need.

2. Attach a male plug to one end, a female plug to the other end. These patent devices come with clear instructions for installation, which is usually accomplished in seconds. The illustration shows several of the many types available.

Note: From here on, we will refer to a "male" plug simply as *plug* and a "female" plug as a *connector*. These are the proper trade terms.

Repairing a Damaged Cord

If one of your extension cords has sustained mechanical damage so that either the insulation or the conductor is severed, it is a simple matter to repair it. If the cut is near one end, simply clip off the damaged section with your wire cutters and install the appropriate plug or connector, making a shorter cord. If the damage is near the middle, cut out the damaged section and make *two* shorter cords by adding plugs and connectors in the appropriate places. (The plugs and connectors removed from commercially produced extension cords cannot usually be reused as they are almost always molded onto the insulation of the cord itself. The patent plugs and connectors you install yourself can be used over and over as necessary.)

Making a Three Wire Extension

Three-wire extension cords are a bit more complex. (A three-wire cord is one that has a separate grounding wire in addition to the hot and neutral wires. It is used for appliances that have three-prong, grounded plugs.)

First of all, there are two different types of three-wire cord available, each with its own system of coding the conductors.

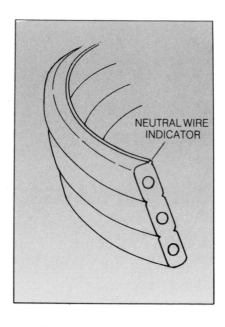

NEUTRAL WIRE INDICATOR

• Flat three-wire cord identifies one of the three conductors by means of an inconspicuous ridge in the plastic insulation (see illustration). This ridge marks the NEUTRAL wire. The middle wire is always used as the GROUND wire and the wire on the opposite side is always used as the HOT wire.

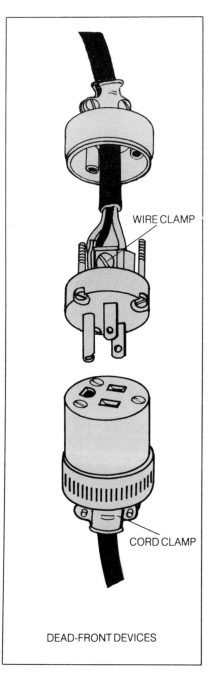

WIRE CLAMP

CORD CLAMP

DEAD-FRONT DEVICES

• Round three-wire cord contains three plastic-insulated conductors, a black wire, a white wire and a green wire, inside an additional rubber or plastic insulator. The coding in this type of wire is traditional: the black is the hot wire, the white the neutral, and the green the ground.

The new Code requires that plugs and connectors for three-wire cords be of the new "dead front" variety. Installation of these devices is considerably more complex than the easy snap-ons made for two-wire cord.

To make a three-wire extension cord, first buy enough (or cut from your own supply enough) cord to make an extension of the length you want. Then, to wire the "dead front" connectors:

1. For a **plug**: Back out, but do not remove, the screws holding the back section and the prong plate together; separate the two pieces of the device. For a **connector**: Back out, but do not remove, the screws holding the top housing and the wiring portion together; separate the two pieces of the device.

2. Carefully cut and strip about 1½ inches of the outer insulation, if you are using round cord, exposing the inner wires. Strip about ½ inch of insulation from the ends of each of the conductors. If you are using flat cord, separate the three conductors for a distance of about 1½ inches and strip about ½ inch of insulation from the end of each.

3. Loosen the cord clamps on both plug and connector and insert one end of the cord into each.

4. The actual method of connection—the securing of the conductors to the terminals of the device—differs somewhat from one manufacturer's product to another. Every device should come with full instructions for proper installation, but the two main methods—clamps and screw terminals—are easily described.

Note that—whether the terminals have screws whose heads hold the wires in place or metal clamping plates secured by screws—one of the three connections will be yellow or gold in color, one will be white, and one green. The gold-colored terminal should be connected to the HOT wire, the white terminal to the NEUTRAL wire, and the green terminal to the GROUND wire (see comments on coding, above).

• **For screw terminals:**
Loosen each of the three terminal screws. Twist the strands of each of the conductors tightly together. (For a handy method of doing this *before* removing the insulation in stripping, see p. 36.) Screws tighten in a clockwise direction. Bend a loop in each of the wires so that the loop will follow the direction of the screw as it is being tightened—clockwise. Making ABSOLUTELY SURE that you are connecting the right wires to the right terminals, secure each wire in turn, slipping the loop around the screw, making sure it fits snugly around the threaded shank of the screw, and tightening the screw securely, making sure that the wire is not forced out from under the screw head while you are tightening it.

• **For clamp terminals:**
Loosen the screws that tighten the clamping plates. Twist the strands of each of the conductors tightly, as above. Making ABSOLUTELY SURE that you are connecting the right wire to

the right connector, insert the exposed end of each wire in turn into its proper clamp and secure by tightening the screw firmly.

5. Securely tighten the **cord clamp** on each device. This prevents mechanical stress from being transferred to the actual conductor-terminal connections.

6. Reassemble the plug and connector by screwing the two halves of each back together.

Repairing a Three-Wire Extension

Repairing a three-wire cord damaged near one end is no different from repairing a two-wire cord except for the procedure involved in attaching the plug or connector. Simply cut the cord near the damaged area, remove the plug or con-nector from the short end and reattach it to the main section of the cord.

If you should be unlucky enough to cut a three-wire cord in the middle of a long run of cable, as happens fairly frequently when using such tools as hedge trimmers outdoors, you may need to make an emergency SPLICE. (According to the Code, extensions should not be spliced; they should consist of a single uninterrupted length of cable. But if you are in the middle of a job, especially if it is a weekend and the hardware store is closed, you may choose this TEMPORARY expedient.)

Splicing

1. Cleanly cut the unplugged cord into two pieces.

2. On a round cord, use your utility knife to carefully remove about 7½ inches of the outer insulation from both of the cut ends.

On a flat cord, separate the wires from each other for a distance of 7½ inches on each piece of cord.

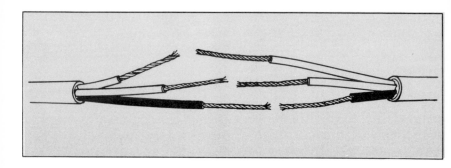

3. Stagger the splices by cutting the individual conductors as follows (see illustration):

• From one cord—Cut off 5 inches of the HOT (black or smooth) wire (see comments on coding, p. 14). Cut off 2½ inches of the GROUND (green or middle) wire.

• From the other cord—Cut off 5 inches of the NEUTRAL (white or "ridged") wire. Cut off 2½ inches of the GROUND (green or middle) wire.

4. Strip off 2 inches of insulation from each of the six wire ends. Also remove any other insulation around them.

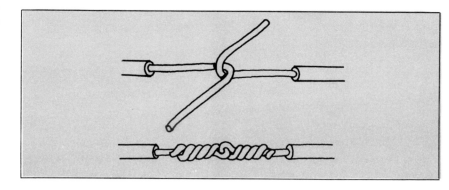

5. Splice the ground wires together (the green to the green or the middle to the middle). Splice the hot wires together (the black to the black or smooth to smooth). Finally, splice the neutral wires together (the white to the white or ridged to ridged). All splices should be done as illustrated.

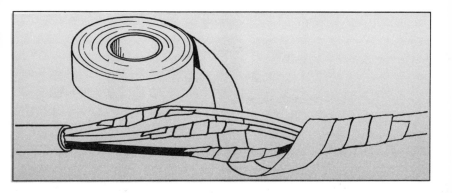

6. Wrap each individual splice well with electrical tape, running the tape at least ½ inch past the bare wires on both sides.

7. Wrap the whole area of the splice with several layers of electrical tape, encompassing the three individual splices.

Separating Extension Cord

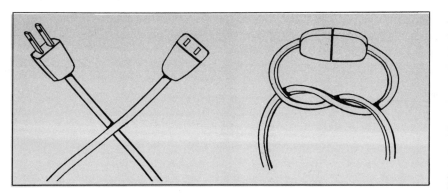

The outlets (female plugs) on heavy duty extension cords seem to have the proclivity for separating from the plugs on tools at the wrong moment. When using a hedge clipper, lawn mower, circular saw, etc., a little too much tension on the connection pulls it apart. There is an easy remedy for this nuisance: tie a loose knot using both the tool cord and extension cord and secure the connectors. The strain will then be focused on the knot rather than the joint and prevent the connection from separating.

Lamps

Although lamps are not all identical in construction, each must have a socket, cord and plug as components. (Most also have a switch that is either part of the socket or part of the cord.) The socket is attached to a threaded tube (*lamp pipe*) in the center of the fixture that holds the entire lamp together; the lamp wires are secured to the socket by screws (*terminals*) and then fed through the tube, out the base, ending in a plug. Some lamps also have a *harp* (the wire frame that the shade rests on); and various other fittings—one or more metal washers, a decorative metal cap, an extension neck, a lead weight, and a felt covering on the underside of the base.

If you have an old lamp with a frayed cord, it should be re-wired; in fact, it is a good idea to replace the plug, too, with one of the new easily-attached types. Although the socket probably works, you might want to replace it with a new one of the same type or one with a three-way switch. You also might want to replace a "stationary" harp with a two-piece detachable one.

If you know where you want the lamp to sit once it is rewired, measure the distance from the wall receptacle to the lamp base area by laying a string along the path that the cord will follow. Measure the length of the string and the height of the lamp from the base to the socket, add an extra 12″ and you will have determined the necessary lamp cord length. (You can always shorten the cord if this measurement is too long.)

Tools and Materials

- screwdriver
- utility knife or wire stripper
- lineman's pliers
- pocket knife
- 18/2 lamp cord
- socket
- plug
- detachable harp
- adhesive

Disassembly

To disassemble: (Not all of the following steps may be necessary for your particular lamp.)

1. Set the *unplugged* lamp on the table.

2. Remove the bulb.

3. Clip the wire in two near the base to facilitate removal.

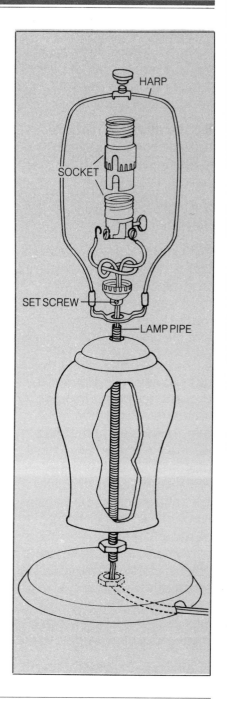

HARP

SOCKET

SET SCREW

LAMP PIPE

4. If the lamp has several extra parts that differ from the illustration, diagram the assembly as it is taken apart (so you won't forget what goes where).

5. If there is felt on the bottom, slip the pocket knife under it to loosen and remove it from the base.

6. If there is a knot in the cord at the base, untie it.

7. If it is necessary to disassemble the body of the lamp from the lamp pipe (it usually is *not*), loosen and remove the nut holding the base to the lamp pipe with the pliers.

8. The word PRESS is stamped on the outer shell of the socket. Put pressure on this spot and try to separate the shell from the cap. If it does not come apart, wedge in a screwdriver to unlock the little notches at the PRESS point. Lift up the outer shell and the cardboard insulation under it. Pull out the mechanical part of the socket—the cord should follow along with it. (It is not absolutely necessary to replace the socket cap on a brass fitting—they all are similar, even though the switching mechanism may differ.) If you do

choose to remove the old cap, loosen the set screw, if there is one, and unthread the cap from the pipe.

9. If you are going to replace the harp, this is the time to lift out the old harp. It may have a threaded washer securing it, or it may simply be held down by the cap.

Reassembly

1. If you are installing a new "detachable" harp (which will later allow you to change harp sizes without taking the whole lamp apart), lift the small sleeves on the new harp top and squeeze to separate it from the harp wings. Slip the wing piece over the pipe and secure it with the threaded washer and/or socket cap (see Step 2).

2. Separate the new socket (if you are not reinstalling the old one). Thread the cap on the pipe and tighten. Secure the set screw.

3. Separate the two wires of the cord for a distance of about 2½ inches.

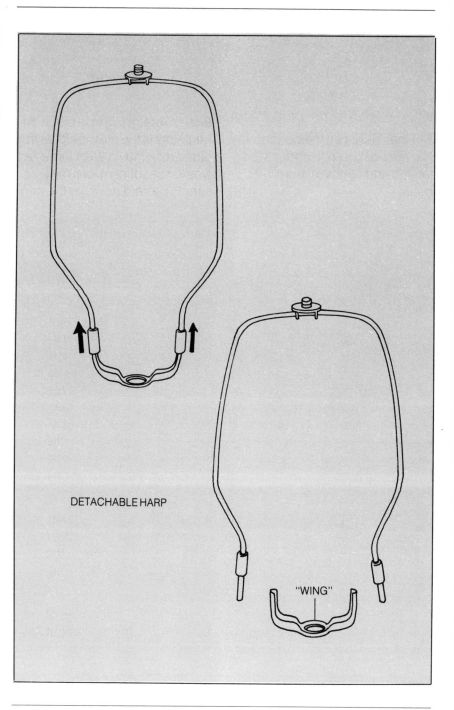

DETACHABLE HARP

"WING"

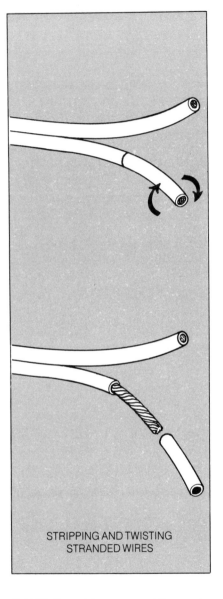

STRIPPING AND TWISTING
STRANDED WIRES

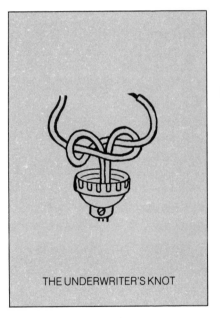

THE UNDERWRITER'S KNOT

tion. Twist the ¾-inch section of insulation in a clockwise direction making two or three turns; it will seem to unthread as it separates from the cord body. The resulting twisted bare stranded wires should each form a tight single wire.

5. Push the uncut end of the cord into the cap and down through the pipe until it feeds through the other end. Pull it through until only six to eight inches are left protruding from the cap.

4. With the strippers, cut through the insulation on each wire ¾ inch from the end. Be careful *not to cut the wire*, only the insula-

6. Using the two wires, tie an **Underwriters knot** (see illustration). Pull the wires firmly to assure a tight compact knot.

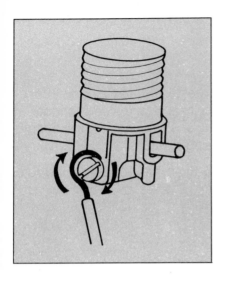

(Step 6) takes up too much room in the cap. If so, remove the wires from the terminal, untie the knot, and clip the wires to about 1½″ long. Repeat Step 4, dispense with the knot, attach the terminals, and snap the socket together.)

9. If the base was removed, re-attach by setting the pipe in the center hole, threading the nut onto the pipe, and tightening with the pliers.

10. If you untied a knot in the cord at the base, tie one now. Slip the cord through the hole in the side of the base and pull to take up the slack, but do not make taut.

11. Cleanly cut the end of the cord wire and attach the plug.

12. Lightly spread a few drops of adhesive on the underside of the lamp base and affix the felt to it. Set the lamp upright.

13. To reassemble the harp: raise the sleeves, squeeze the lower section of the springy top, insert it into the wings, and lock in by sliding the sleeves back down.

14. Replace the bulb and insert the plug into an outlet. Turn ON the switch and Eureka, you have light!

7. Loosen, but do not remove, the two terminal screws on the threaded portion of the socket. Bend the bare wires into a clockwise loop as shown. Slip each wire under one of the terminal screws. (It doesn't matter which wire goes to which terminal.) Use the tip of the screwdriver to wrap the wire snugly around the screw shank—there should be no stray exposed wires. Tighten the screws.

8. Pull on the cord at the bottom of the tube to draw the excess wire through the lamp pipe. Position the insulator over the socket and push the outer shell into the cap. The parts should snap together audibly. (You may find that you can't reassemble the socket because the knot

Light Fixtures

Now that you have wired a lamp, you should be ready to tackle a slightly more challenging job: replacing a wall- or ceiling-mounted light fixture. Once you understand the basics, you'll be able to deal with *any* fixture.

Tools and Materials

- screwdriver
- pliers
- test light (pigtail or neon)
- wire nuts
- six-foot ladder
- new fixture

Disconnecting the Old Fixture

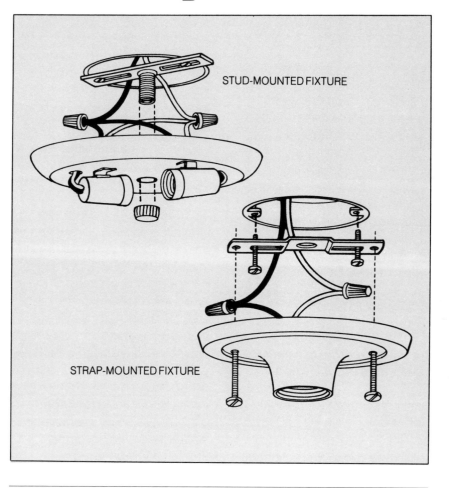

STUD-MOUNTED FIXTURE

STRAP-MOUNTED FIXTURE

1. First, *kill the circuit* supplying the fixture.

2. Climb the ladder and remove the fixture "canopy." The two most common methods of attachment are illustrated here. Either remove the two mounting screws with your screwdriver *or* remove the cap nut in the center of the fixture, using pliers if necessary to loosen the nut.

3. Draw the fixture down away from the ceiling or out away from the wall. This will reveal an outlet box mounted flush with the wall or ceiling surface (see p. 39). Most light fixtures are mounted over round or octagonal outlet boxes, but other shapes are occasionally used. Also revealed will be some—or many —wires. Getting these wires sorted out may be slightly confusing at first, but we'll go through the possibilities one step at a time. DO NOT TOUCH ANY WIRES AT THIS TIME. First, let's take a *look*.

• There will *always* be at least two wires *from the fixture itself*. If the fixture has a single socket, there will be TWO. If the fixture has more than one socket, there will be one *pair* of wires for each socket. The wires leading from the fixture socket will not neces-

sarily be coded black and white like house wires, but they will be coded in some way; one will have a stripe, for example, so that it can be distinguished from the other.

• There will be at least two house wires entering the box from inside the wall or ceiling.

• If the light fixture is operated by a wall switch there will almost certainly be more than two wires leading into the box from inside the wall or ceiling. The same is true if the fixture happens to be in the middle of a circuit—if the wires go on from this outlet box to feed other devices.

• In some cases, wires may be connected together in groups of three or *more*.

Let's take a detailed look at a typical ceiling box. *If* your house has been correctly wired, one of the leads from the fixture socket will go to a wire or group of wires, *all* of which are white. The other lead will usually go to a single house wire, which may be white or black. If this wire is white, it *should* have a dab of black paint on the end of the insulation. Finally, there may be a group of black house wires to which the socket leads are not connected at all. In some cases, one of

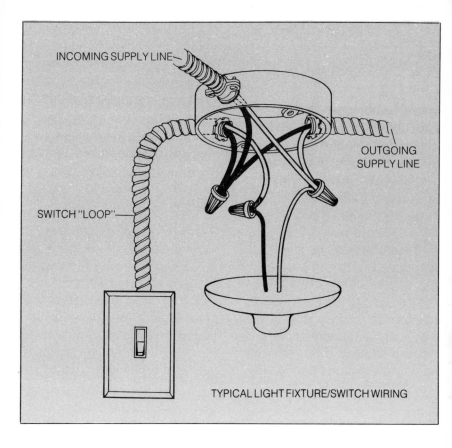

INCOMING SUPPLY LINE

OUTGOING SUPPLY LINE

SWITCH "LOOP"

TYPICAL LIGHT FIXTURE/SWITCH WIRING

these *may* be white but, again, should have a dab of black paint on the end of the insulation.

Explanation: This most typical light fixture feeding and switching brings *three* cables into the box: one bringing current in from the supply, one carrying current on to another device further along down the circuit, one acting as a "loop" to the wall switch.

• The white neutral wires will be connected to form a continuous neutral, and *one of the leads* from the socket will be connected to them.

• The black hot wires will also be connected to form a continuous circuit to feed the next outlet.

• *One* of the two wires leading to the wall switch will be connected to the hot, black house wires. The *other* lead from the fixture socket will be connected to the remaining wire leading to the switch. (Power runs from the incoming hot wire down to the switch. If the switch is then turned on [closed] power will run back up the other wire in the cable running between the wall switch and the ceiling box which is connected to the remaining lead from the fixture socket. This forms the complete circuit that lights the bulb in the fixture.)

The problem, as far as coding is concerned (remember here that *all* wires that carry hot power are supposed to be black), is that standard two wire cable always contains one black wire and one white wire, so one of the wires in the switch "loop" will always be incorrectly coded. The proper solution to this is to paint the end of the white wire black to indicate that it is a hot wire. In practical terms, it makes absolutely no difference which end of the switch loop is connected to the hot house wires in the ceiling box and which is connected to the lead from the fixture. Many electricians do not bother to paint the white wire black, however, and that can cause considerable confusion.

With all that in mind, the importance of the first two disconnection steps should be clear.

1. Identify the wires leading from the fixture socket(s).

2. Make note of which wires or groups of wires they are connected to. These are the *only* wires you will concern yourself with. In connecting the new fixture you must be sure to connect the socket leads to the same wires you are about to disconnect the old ones from.

3. If the wires are all clustered together, separate the black set from the white set by pushing them away from one another, *touching only the insulated part of the wires. NEVER let the bare house wires touch each other or the box.* (They shouldn't be bare yet, but it's not too early to be thinking about safety.)

4. One at a time, remove the tape or wire nut from each of the connections of fixture socket wires to house wires. *Do not touch the bare wires with your hands once the insulators are off.*

5. Now TEST to be absolutely certain the power is off. Turn the wall switch to the ON position. If you are not absolutely sure that the bulb in your pigtail tester is working, verify that fact by trying the bulb in some lamp that you know to be working. Perform the following THREE tests.

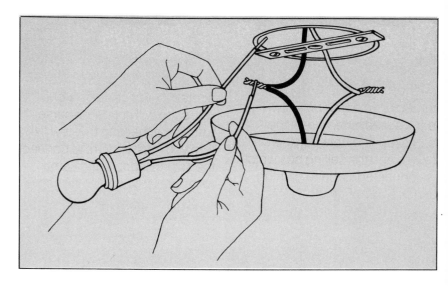

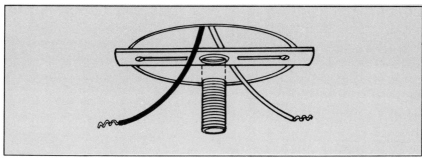

a) Touch the two leads (wires) of the pigtail simultaneously to the bare black wire and the box,

b) to the bare white wire and the box,

c) to the bare black and white wires simultaneously.

If the bulb lights during ANY of these tests, the power is not off. Recheck the panel box and test again until you are SURE that

the power is disconnected.

Once you are sure that the power is off, separate the house wires from the fixture wires. Untwist one socket wire from the circuit wire or group of wires. Next hold the fixture with one hand and detach the remaining connection. (You'll be left with two bare wires or groups of wires protruding out of the box and the fixture sitting in your hand.)

Mounting the New Fixture

Fixtures with Two Mounting Holes

Depending on the spacing of the holes—if they do not line up with the "ears" on the box—you may need a **mounting strap** (also known as a **crossbar**). A mounting strap should be packaged with the new fixture along with the required mounting screws.

1. In a box with ears, secure the strap to the ears with short screws.

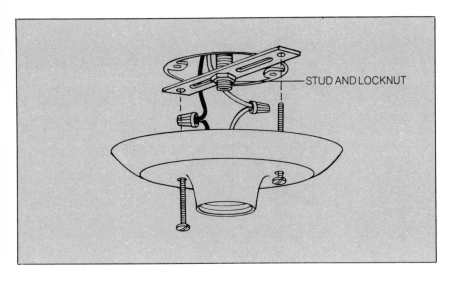

STUD AND LOCKNUT

2. In a box without ears you will find a "stud" affixed in the center. Mount the strap over the stud, securing it with a locknut.

Fixtures with a Center Hole

If the box has a **stud**, you may simply be able to mount the canopy, securing it by screwing on the ornamental locknut.

If the stud is not long enough, or if the thread size doesn't fit the locknut, you will have to lengthen the stud and/or change the thread size by means of a reducing nut or *hickey*, devices that accommodate different-sized threads in their top and bottom portions. A

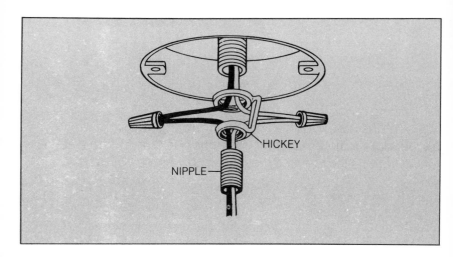

nipple (a short piece of threaded pipe) of the right thread size will be screwed into the bottom portion of the reducing nut or hickey. Take your locknut with you to the electrical supply house to be sure of getting the right size nipple and the right size reducing nut or hickey.

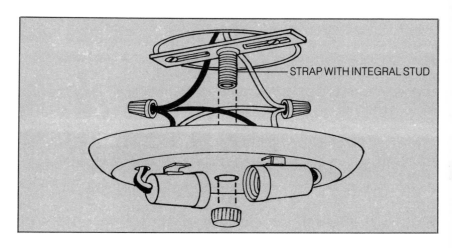

If the box lacks a stud altogether, you can purchase either a strap with a stud integrally mounted on it or with a central hole, threaded to accept a nipple. The former type of strap is illustrated here, the latter on p. 49. In either case, the strap is mounted to the box with short screws securing it to the box ears.

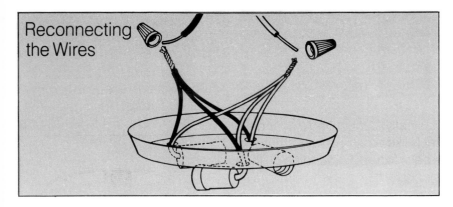

Reconnecting
the Wires

In actuality, it is not critical which of the wires leading from the fixture socket goes to which house wire, especially if it is a single-socket fixture. What *is* critical is that in a multiple socket fixture all of the same-coded wires go to the *same* respective house wires. In other words, if each socket has a pair of wires, say one black and one black with a white stripe, all of the black socket wires should be connected *together* to one of the house wires and all the white-striped wires should be connected *together* to the other. With this principle in mind, proceed as follows:

1. Wrap the stranded black wire(s) from the fixture socket around the bare black house wire (or group of wires) from which you earlier disconnected one of the leads from the old fixture socket; wrap the stranded black-with-white-stripe (or whatever the coding is) wires around the other white, bare house wire from which you earlier disconnected the other lead from the old fixture socket. Secure the connections by threading on wire nuts in the clockwise direction.

2. Make sure all connections are neat and tidy—no bare wires straggling out of the wire nuts. Then push all the wires back up into the box, bending them as necessary to get them to fit.

3. Attach the fixture to the wall or ceiling using the appropriate mounting hardware.

4. Insert bulb(s) into socket(s). Turn the wall switch (or fixture switch, if there is no wall switch) to OFF. Return power to the circuit (turn the circuit back ON). Your new fixture should light up when you switch it on.

Hanging a Chandelier

Basically, connecting a chandelier is like putting up any other type of fixture. Depending on the electrical box design, canopy width, weight of the unit, and material used for suspension (chain or heavy cord), various fittings are used to fasten the fixture to the ceiling. Most new chandeliers have installation diagrams and instructions included in their packaging; however, they usually don't have all the necessary fittings for securing the fixture to the particular ceiling box in your house. You'll find that you don't have a hickey with the right diameter for the box stud; a shorter or longer nipple is needed for the thread of the screw-nut loop assembly (the part of that chain is attached to), the new canopy is not deep enough for the fittings you have, etc. (The installation of a new canopy onto a very old box almost always calls for more or different fittings.) Don't be surprised if a trip or two to the hardware store or lamp supply house is required. Be sure to take all of the fittings that you do have with you when additional parts are called for. Note which fittings "fit" and which do not.

Tools and materials are the same as those used for securing a ceiling fixture.

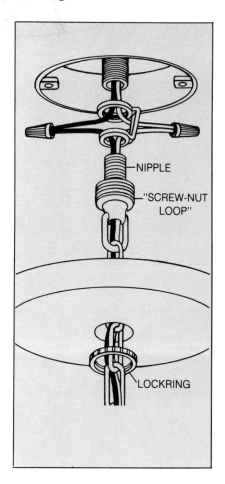

NIPPLE

"SCREW-NUT LOOP"

LOCKRING

• Most chandliers are supported by a hickey that is threaded over the box's stud (see illustration).

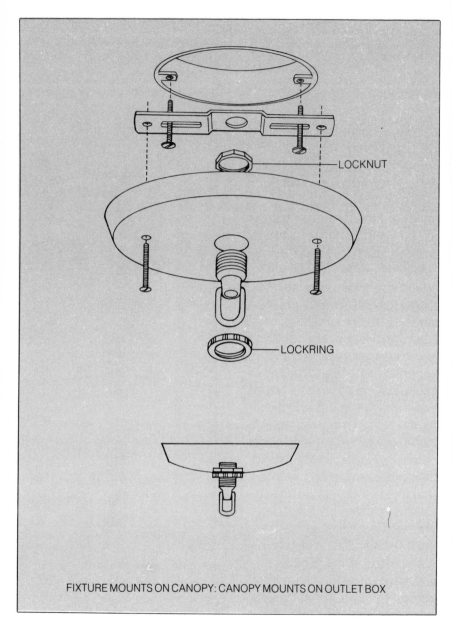

LOCKNUT

LOCKRING

FIXTURE MOUNTS ON CANOPY: CANOPY MOUNTS ON OUTLET BOX

• Lightweight fixtures, if they have two screw holes in the canopy, can be attached to a strap.

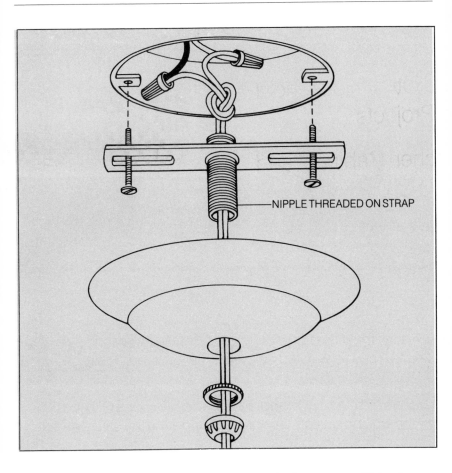

NIPPLE THREADED ON STRAP

• Units that are suspended by a cord also are lightweight but are secured differently. The cord is threaded up through a nipple and then has a knot tied in it.   .

• A fixture heavier than 50 pounds should be hung by an electrician. It *must* be supported independently of the box.

Of course, to begin, the present fixture has to be removed. Turn OFF the power and go to work. Refer to page 40 for fixture disconnection, and then look at the diagrams on pages 47-49 for the specific chandelier that you have. Hanging a suspended unit is not difficult; the only problem you might encounter is that you don't have enough hands to support the unit and connect it at the same time. Working with a partner will make the job quicker and easier.

Wall Switches

Today there is a large variety of wall switches on the market. Those listed below are the four types most commonly used.

• The old standard **toggle** switch noisily snaps ON and OFF. A modernized quieter version of the toggle is the "quiet switch." It doesn't make the obvious sound of the older toggle.

• A colorful decorator line of devices with a large **rocker** switch is being produced by several manufacturers. Included in its package is a specially designed cover plate that fits the switch.

• The **dimmer** switch has either a rotary control knob or a toggle handle. Some units have high-low light regulation while others have continuous range (up to 600 watts). A dimmer does not have the life expectancy of other switches, and it is priced higher than other switches, but it allows you to conserve electricity when high illumination is not necessary. (A *special* dimmer is required for fluorescent lighting.)

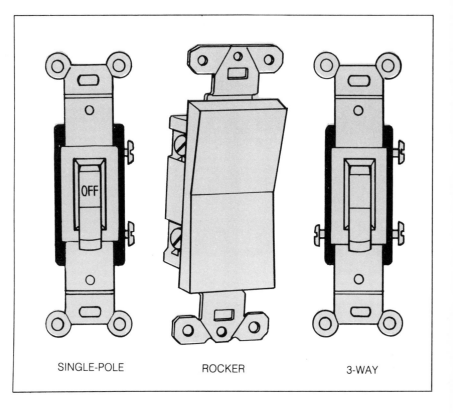

| SINGLE-POLE | ROCKER | 3-WAY |

After you've chosen one of the four types, you'll choose one of these options:

• A single-pole switch (one switch controls one fixture or receptacle) has two terminals.

• A three-way switch (two switches control one device from different locations) has three terminals.

When using a dimmer for a three-way switch, only one three-way dimmer is called for; the other switch does not have to be replaced. Do not use a dimmer in a four-way application unless you have an electrician install it.

Connecting a switch to the house wiring is not difficult. In a single-pole device, screw terminals can be placed in one of several locations on the body of the switch. Terminal placement is a whim of the manufacturer and has no bearing on the performance of the switch.

There is another type of connection called *back-wiring* (see illustration, page 54). Some, but not all, devices offer this in addition to screw terminals, as an added convenience. Instead of using a wire loop secured to the terminal with a screw, the wire is "plugged" into a terminal hole.

Most dimmers use neither screw nor plug-in terminals. Instead, stranded lead wires and wire nuts (provided with the device) are employed for making connnections.

Tools and Materials

- screwdriver
- utility knife
- test light
- lineman's pliers
- long-nose pliers
- wire strippers (if using back-wiring)
- pocket screwdriver (if using back wiring)
- new switch

Disconnecting the Old Switch

1. Kill the circuit supplying the fixture.

2. Remove the screws holding the switch plate against the wall. (If the plate is painted to the wall, run the knife blade around the perimeter and then pry off.) Tape the screws to the plate and set aside.

3. Loosen the two long screws that hold the switch to the box tabs — withdraw the screws from the tabs but not from the device. Pull the switch out of the box.

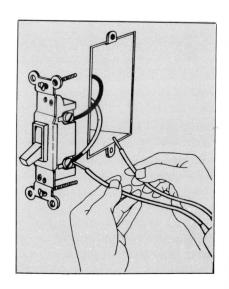

4. Test the connections to be sure that the circuit is OFF. With the wires of the test lamp, there are two combinations to check: touch the box and one terminal screw, then the box and the other screw (see illustration, page 99). In a back-wired connection: touch the box and spring release slot (small rectangular cutouts next to the round terminal holes) adjacent to the secured wire, then the box and the other wire slot. The bulb should not light during any of these test combinations. If it does, the proper circuit was not shut off. Recheck the panel box.

5. Once you are sure that the current is off, in a three-way switch, tag the "common" wire with a piece of tape. It can be identified as follows: it will be connected to a different-colored (usually copper-colored) terminal screw than the other two, OR the terminal to which it is connected will be marked with the word COMMON or COM. In back-wiring, it will be plugged into the slot directly adjacent to the common screws or labeled COMMON.

6. Disconnect the wires from the device.

For screw connections: loosen the screws and slide off the wire loops. This may take a little effort. Pry the loops further open with the long-nose pliers or a screwdriver.

In a plug-in connection: insert the blade of a small screwdriver into the release slots to move the spring that clamps the wire to the device, pulling out the wire at the same time.

7. When you're selecting your new switch, look for a unit that is packaged on a card with specific installation directions. Check with a salesperson to insure that you obtain the correct device for the circuit. (A three-way switch must be replaced with a three-way, a single-pole with a single-pole, etc.)

If you have aluminum wiring, you must use a device specifically indicated for use with aluminum wire. It should carry the stamped code, CO/ALR, on the mounting strap.

Installing the New Switch

For a screw connection:

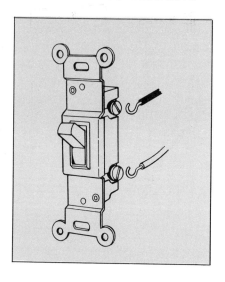

Single-pole switch. Slip the house wire loops under the screw heads and tighten. The loops might need to be closed slightly with pliers to fit snugly under the screws. It is not critical which wire goes to which terminal. (See page 41 for an explanation of switch loops.)

Three-way switch. Secure the tagged wire to the terminal marked COMMON and then affix the other two wires to the other two terminals.

For a plug-in connection:

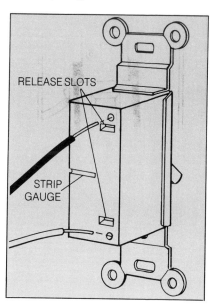

RELEASE SLOTS

STRIP GAUGE

1. Clip the ends of the house wires, removing the old loops. Hold the switch with the back facing you. Note a depression in the plastic labeled STRIP GAUGE. Strip the house wire to this required length. Then, simply push the wires into the terminal holes making connections as described above for the screw type terminal connection.

2. Make sure no bare wires are exposed; then fold the wires back into the box.

3. Secure the device to the box ears with the screws provided in the mounting slots.

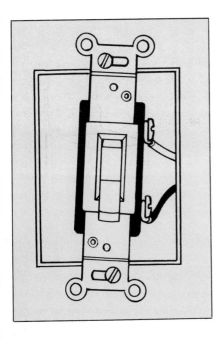

Installing a Dimmer Switch

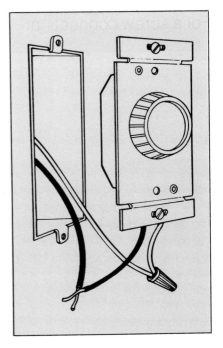

4. If the box is slightly askew, loosen the mounting screws and reposition the device.

5. Replace the cover plate and secure to the device with screws.

6. Flip the switch to the OFF position and then turn the current back on. Activate the switch to see that it works properly. In a single-pole toggle switch, if you find that the light is on when the handle is in the downward position, you have installed the switch upside down. Shut off the circuit and reverse the orientation of the device in the box. Close up as before.

1. Straighten out the loop in the house wire and snip to leave about ⅜ inch of bare wire.

2. Wrap the stranded wires of the dimmer around the bare house wires and cover with wire nuts. (Remember that the common wire in a three-way switch will have different color insulation than the other two.)

3. Follow steps 2-6 above.

Receptacles

Most receptacle devices (you probably call them "wall outlets") in a home are the **duplex** kind—two outlets in one device. You might also have a few single specialized receptacles to which an air conditioner, clothes dryer, or range are connected.

Receptacles are made in the usual ivory and brown; they also are being produced now in a companion line to decorator switches. All duplex outlets now have three slots. They can be electrified by side-wiring or back-wiring (see Switches, page 54). The device has a set of terminals for each of the two outlets plus one hexagonal green grounding screw. Take a close look at a receptacle: one slot is shorter than the other. The shorter slot is the hot wire side and the longer slot is the neutral wire side. (This distinction was not made in some old two-slot units.) The round hole (slot) is connected to the grounding wire.

The Code now requires that all receptacle devices be grounded to the electrical boxes to which they are secured. Years ago this was not the case. Of course, by looking at an outlet you can't tell if the box is really grounded or not. The older type of two-slot receptacle did not have a grounding wire attached to it. With a system wired with armored cable, if the box was grounded, the device was automatically grounded to the box and cover plate by the fact that it was a metal-to-metal connection. If you have two-slot outlets, it is easy to check to see whether the receptacle is grounded.

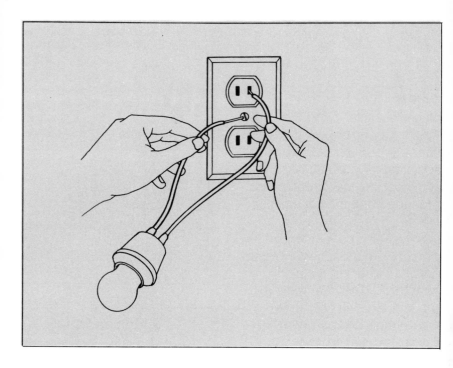

Testing for a Grounded Receptacle in a Two-Slot device

Insert one wire of a test lamp into the shorter (hot) slot and touch the other wire to the screw holding the cover plate to the device (see illustration above.) The bulb should light. If it does on this test, the outlet is indeed grounded. If the bulb does not light, test the longer neutral slot and the screw. If the bulb lights, the wires might be reversed in the outlet (or they could be reversed throughout the entire circuit). *Call an electrician to check out the line.* In a duplex receptacle, remember to test both outlets since it is possible that more than one circuit may be feeding the device. (If you live in a very old house in which the wiring has not been updated, do not be surprised if the bulb does not light when the slots are tested. The circuits in all probability are not grounded.)

Attaching an Adapter Plug

If your home has only the two-slot receptacles, you'll frequently need to attach a three-prong plug to an outlet. NEVER pull out the third prong on a plug. Purchase an adapter plug made specifically for this purpose. If you know that the receptacle is grounded and the adapter is installed correctly, the tool or appliance being connected will be properly grounded. If your box is not grounded, installing an adapter plug will not create a grounded outlet, but it *will* at least enable a three-prong plug to be used in a two-slot receptacle.

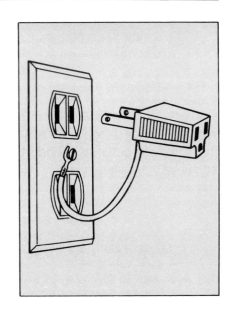

Testing for a Grounded Receptacle in a Three-Slot Device

The round hole in a three-slot device tells you that it is a unit that should definitely be grounded. To be *sure*, insert a test lamp wire into the grounding slot and the shorter hot slot. If the bulb doesn't light, *call an electrician*. Something was not wired correctly.

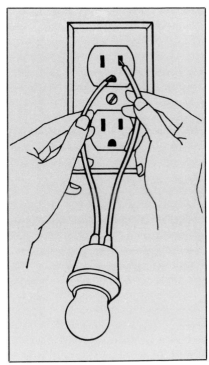

Replacing a Receptacle

When you have tested and know that a two-slot outlet is grounded and want to replace it with a three-slot unit, this can be done easily.

Tools and Materials

• screwdriver

• test lamp

• long-nose pliers

• lineman's pliers

• wire strippers (if back wiring)

• pocket screwdriver (if back-wiring)

• grounded receptacle

• 1 foot No. 14 green insulated grounding wire

• 10/24 or 10/32 ½-inch machine screws

Disconnecting the Old Receptacle

1. Kill the circuit supplying the receptacle.

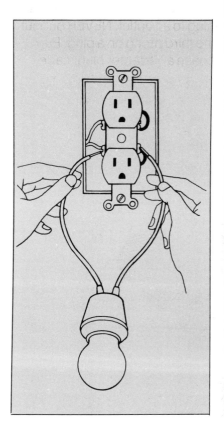

2. Test the device to be sure that the power is off. Remove the cover plate and tape the screw to it. Touch the wires of the test lamp to one pair of terminals as shown in the illustration **above**. If the bulb lights, recheck the panel box. The power is not off.

3. Once you are *sure* the power is off, loosen the two long screws holding the device to the box tabs. Withdraw the screws from the tabs but not from the unit. Pull the receptacle out of the box. You will find two or more wires affixed to the unit depending on the location of the device within the run of the circuit (or if two circuits lead to the outlets). To make wiring the new new receptacle easy, diagram the present wiring *before* you disconnect anything, indicating which wire led to which terminal. Then tag each wire (e.g. white wire attached to upper silver screw, black wire attached to lower brass screw, etc.)

4. Loosen the terminal screws and remove the wires.

5. Take the old unit to the store, and purchase a new grounded receptacle. *If you have aluminum wiring, you must use a device specifically indicated for use with aluminum wire. It should carry the stamped code, CO/ALR, on the mounting strap.*

Connecting the New Receptacle

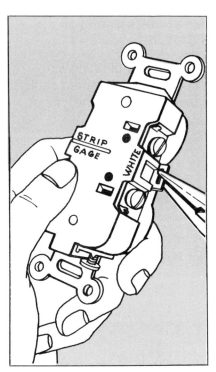

1. Examine the old device. On a unit that used current from two *separate* circuits (called a two-circuit receptacle), you will notice that the break-off or terminal fin tabs between the two pairs of terminals will have been removed (see illustration). If the new device is also to be a two-circuit receptacle, use a screwdriver or pliers to remove the break-off tab on both sides of the device.

2. Cut a six-inch piece of the No. 14 wire. Strip ¾ inch off each end. With the long-nose pliers, form a clockwise loop on one end.

3. Attach the grounding wire.

For a box with armored cable: Make a loop at the other end of the wire. Secure one loop to the back of the **box** with a machine screw. (The screw thread size, either 10/24 or 10/32, depends on the tapped size in the "grounding screw" *hole* in the back of the box.) Slip the other loop under the green grounding screw and secure.

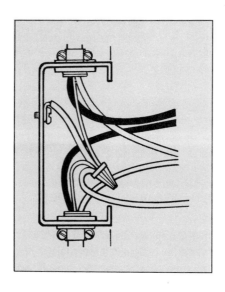

For a box with a nonmetal-sheathed cable: Remove the wire nut or tape covering the

cable grounding-wire splice. With the lineman's pliers wrap the bare straight end of the green wire around the splice (there will now be four wires twisted together) and cover with a wire nut. Secure the looped end of the green wire to the green terminal of the receptacle.

4. Choose which type of attachment you will use for the house wires — screw terminal-wiring or back-wiring (see Switches, page 54), and then secure the wires to the receptacle following the diagram you drew previously.

5. Fold the wires back into the box.

6. Secure the receptacle to the box ears with the long screws provided in the mounting slots.

7. If the box is slightly askew, loosen the mounting screws and straighten it (see illustration on page 55).

8. Replace the outlet cover plate and tighten the screw.

9. Turn the circuit back on.

10. Test the outlet as before for grounding.

Directions for replacing a broken three-slot receptacle are the same as above.

When to Call an Electrician

Although the National Electrical Code is supposed to be followed to the letter, many homes have not been correctly wired or have not been electrically updated. Correct wire coding of insulation may not have been maintained; incorrect wire gauges may have been used in a number of installations; receptacles may not be grounded. Sometimes the wiring system has been tampered with by so many amateur electricians that when you, the rank novice, want to do some electrical work, no wires are the color they should be, the supposed "hot" wire is not "hot," etc. If you run into these problems, forget trying to be an electrical do-it-yourselfer and CALL A LICENSED ELECTRICIAN.

Also call for help when:

• You are afraid of working with electricity or not quite sure of which wires goes where.

• The wire you thought should be in a box is not.

• You open a box and find crumbling insulation around the house wires.

• There is not enough house wire in a box to make a secure connection.

• A fuse repeatedly blows or a circuit breaker continually trips.

• The wall or ceiling area adjacent to an electrical device feels warm.

• You open a box and find charred insulation around the wires.

• All the devices and fixtures in a room are on a single circuit.

The Wallaby Home Care Guides

How to Fix a Leak and Other Household Plumbing Projects

How to Redo Your Kitchen Cabinets and Counter Tops

How to Wallpaper

How to Paint Interiors

How to Build a Deck

How to Wire Electrical Outlets, Switches and Lights

The Wallaby Auto Care Guides

How to Tune Your Chevy Chevette

How to Tune Your Toyota Corolla